WHAT IN THE WORLD? BRIEF OBSERVATIONS OF THE HUMAN CONDITION and WHERE DO WE GO FROM HERE?

2nd Edition

Edwin Jay Sparkes

Grosvenor House
Publishing Limited

All rights reserved
First published by Austin Macauley Publishers Ltd. 2014
This Second edition published 2024
Copyright © Edwin Jay Sparkes, 2014 and 2024

The right of Edwin Jay Sparkes to be identified as the author of
this work has been asserted in accordance with Section 78
of the Copyright, Designs and Patents Act 1988

The book cover is copyright to Edwin Jay Sparkes

This book is published by
Grosvenor House Publishing Ltd
Link House
140 The Broadway, Tolworth, Surrey, KT6 7HT.
www.grosvenorhousepublishing.co.uk

This book is sold subject to the conditions that it shall not, by way of
trade or otherwise, be lent, resold, hired out or otherwise circulated
without the author's or publisher's prior consent in any form of
binding or cover other than that in which it is published and
without a similar condition including this condition being
imposed on the subsequent purchaser.

A CIP record for this book
is available from the British Library

First edition: ISBN 78-1-78455-337-1
First published (2014)
Austin Macauley Publishers Ltd.
25 Canada Square, Canary Wharf, London E14 5LB

Second Edition
ISBN 978-1-83615-044-2
eBook ISBN 978-1-83615-045-9

Contents

Introduction	1
1. Money	3
2. Race	7
3. Religion	11
4. Politics	15
5. Health	19
6. Sexuality	23
7. War	25
Where do we go from here?	27
8. Four Examples of Truth and Hope	29
9. A most Unlikely/Unusual Manifesto	33
10. So Where Do We Go From Here?	37
In Closing	41

Acknowledgements

> I have seen that in any great
> undertaking, it is not enough for
> a man to depend simply upon himself.
>
> Lone man (Isna La Wica)
> Teton Sioux[1]

I would like to thank all those whose interest and encouragement which helped immensely to complete this work. Most of all I would like to thank all the writers, researchers and documentary filmmakers of both past and present whose skills and talents in writing and researching that by far exceed mine but nevertheless inspired me to create this book.

---

[1] *Sioux quotes and words of wisdom found at:*
https://www.aaanativearts.com/sioux/sioux-quotes.htm

Introduction

Words have been used in all ways for all purposes. Who amongst us can claim that they have not been influenced (for both good and bad) by a piece of music, poetry, film or an opinion on any topic through social media platforms? Or felt sickened by anger fuelled rhetoric from those who used words to convince others of their supposed truth? Or maybe felt empowered and/or enlightened by a heartfelt and passionate speech which expresses the value of truth, justice and dignity for all people as well as our environment and our future?

To communicate can be a gift or a curse, especially when trying to convey uncomfortable or controversial facts, statistics or points of view even when backed by verifiable evidence and historical examples which give legitimacy to the points being expressed.

Resistance to any real progress is being delayed or halted completely by those who for whatever reason they find valid or comfortable to maintain current situations regardless of disastrous outcomes which affect us all.

> When truth is known yet
> covered in lies, how dark
> lies become and how brightly
> truth shines

1
Money

Of all the weapons human beings have devised to kill, enslave or to force authority and control over each other one beats them all: Money. It has been observed that money (or at least the desire for it) makes people act on some if not all of our most selfish, cruel and negative impulses. A brief list could include fraud, theft, murder and corruption.

The influence that finance has and continues to have on human affairs can and should be measured in suffering. From the genocide of native tribes worldwide (which sadly continues to the present day) to the horrific present-day practice of human trafficking for slave labour and sexual exploitation, the seeking of personal or group profit has been the primary cause and/or it's most common excuse.

How ironic it is that in the so called civilised world the latest electronic device or wearing of gold or other precious metals decorated with yet more precious metals and gemstones are viewed as symbols of affluence and success, whereas if you were to visit many of the regions of the world where these materials are sourced they are usually viewed as symbols of oppression, low standards of living, corruption, civil war and inhumane treatment. It is clear that to many the concept of profit has all but destroyed the idea that another human being's life and dignity are worth more than an item of jewellery, clothing, furniture, electronics or the raw materials required to manufacture them.

Many have heard the phrase "A fool and their money are soon parted," but can this seriously be taken to mean that the selfish and the greedy are more intelligent? Could it also be taken to mean that all the taxes we pay to our bloated, decadent and corrupt institutions are an act of a supreme collective foolishness?

Of all the empires that have come and gone of all the factors that have resulted in their downfall, money combined with its value and its distribution among the population has always been at the forefront of civil unrest, revolutions and eventual collapse. On a more individual level money influences personal attitudes towards other people in various ways, as an example how do you view someone who is homeless and living on the street? Like many do you try your best not to notice them? Or maybe wondered about at least the circumstances which led to them being there?

It is becoming ever more apparent that the failures of our financial system are out in the open for all to see (closed factories, shops, rising prices, tax increases, falling living standards etc), with mistrust growing towards the current system it seems that simple reforms or alternatives are being viewed with similar and equal suspicion.

Lately it also seems that the only groups or individuals who want the current system to continue are those in the position to benefit the most from it while everyone else struggles on a daily basis to maintain what many would consider a basic dignified living standard. If anyone wanted to discuss or bring about real and positive change could they go wrong by using basic morality as a forum for changing our out of date and inhumane debt-based money system?

2
Race

The ways in which people identify or define themselves are becoming ever more aggressive bringing with them dangerous and self-centred opinions and attitudes often resulting in violent and divisive actions.

Everything from our country of birth, political affiliations, clothing choice, gender/identity, social standing (this inevitably throws in the class system as well) all of these and more are being utilised and exploited by those who wish to divide people, and not just on the basis of mere skin colour or ethnicity.

This concept can be seen as quite confusing and rather amusing when we consider the idea that in our world many other species express themselves in many shapes, sizes and indeed colours.

To de-humanise others requires that you first de-humanise yourself. When any group decides to attack another misconception and bigotry always follow one another to an inevitable conclusion of suffering for all. The idea of taking the easiest and most obvious difference between people and make it a moral, spiritual or political issue could be seen as nothing more than an expression of egotism and/or blind anger, which carries with it the potential to spread mistrust, division and polarising attitudes and opinions while free speech and honest debate are denounced/ignored by those who use violence (and the threat of violence) to achieve social and/or political gain. The dangers this presents cannot be ignored as a misguided claim of superiority over others continues to be an undeniable component of history and of the present (empires as an example relied heavily on this concept).

Groups and entire nations have fallen victim to this idea and through that have forced compliance and servitude on so called inferior groups or races. How ironic is it that those who claim superiority require slaves or servants? Isn't it fair to ask that if they're so much better than others <u>why</u> would they even need such people?

Division amongst people has usually caused unrest and destruction whereas unity has tended to build, create and sustain our world (this is of course heavily reliant on genuine moral direction). Right now it is clear which one of these concepts is being utilised more than the other, which poses some very profound and uncomfortable questions such as:

> How long can this situation continue?
> Who benefits from it?
> What kind of person promotes it?
> What kind of environment creates and sustains it?
> Who is willing to confront and resolve it?

On a basic human level we as social beings have a deep need to belong and to feel included, understood or merely to feel welcome within any social group. So called "hate groups" exploit this human attribute to attract new members and to retain current members within their sphere of influence (and therefore control). The term "race traitor" has much relevance in this regard.

When all any person has known or has been exposed to is hatred, bigotry, fear and ignorance, it's quite possible that this will be passed on to the future generations therefore continuing the same hatreds and prejudices that have destroyed countless lives and cultures everywhere. We in our present-day modern world have a tendency to look down upon or judge past generations and civilisations for their misguided and short-sighted mistakes, while continuing to make similar mistakes that brought about their demise. History repeating itself, or is it just us? If any outlook of arrogance and hatred that needs to be recognised as a social and psychological poison then surely the concept of racism is one of the most critical to solve. To confront this problem, many would agree that to resolve said racism with divisive and militant attitudes expressed through destruction of private and public property, violence, threats of violence, infantile name calling and accusations and other destructive behaviour, will only lead to wider divisions where they exist, while potentially creating new ones where none existed before. Also, that actions such as these could be used to reinforce or justify extremist views and actions of individuals and groups on both sides of the issue while perpetuating contempt from the vast majority of people who merely wish to live in peace with all other people regardless of their skin colour.

There is only one race of people on the earth. We call ourselves the human race. This invites a choice to each of us.

Do you want to be part of its stability to promote peace, prosperity and growth for all people or be part of its destruction? This choice is yours as an individual to make and no one else's.

3
Religion

The individuals right to have faith/belief in any of the many spiritual and philosophical practices and traditions has and continues to be one of the most fought for expressions of personal choice and freedom that humanity has engaged in. There is of course a very good reason for this as it plays a major role in personal and cultural identity, and that it is also one of the many branches of liberty that we as human beings value.

Persecution of one religious group by another is possibly one of the most undeniable factors that have shaped cultural and individual attitudes within society. With large migrations of groups from one area to another (or individuals on personal spiritual journeys) written about in many spiritual texts and history books, is it not possible that fear, disagreement or misunderstanding of unstudied and therefore unknown religious practices be one of the root causes of past and present turmoil and violence? The most brutal of conflicts generally have spiritual/religious beliefs as the most unifying concepts to provide common ground to any group seeing itself suffering from persecution (when combined with extremist nationalistic attitudes and outlooks of superiority the outcome can be much worse). It's a terrible irony that violent and oppressive behaviour performed in the name of any faith, deity or spiritual teaching instantly devalues those teachings inviting contempt, division and mistrust.

Any study of the many avenues of spiritual and religious disciplines makes it very easy to see more similarities between the many faiths than there are differences, yet all faiths claim in varying degrees to be the one true path to what is referred to be divine. This can of course be a very dangerous, egocentric and self-defeating process risking harm to many.

Many of us at some point in our lives pondered life and its meaning in order to attain a more personally profound understanding of the world, life in general and our place within it. This is one of the unique traits that we as human beings have as it expresses our ability to see and to reflect upon concepts and ideas from many sides and perspectives not just for individuals understanding, but to also reflect upon the reasoning of others. Many times during any aggressive social or political uprising it's usually spiritual leaders and those of learning that are most persecuted (and sometimes co-opted) within any group. If anything could provide evidence of how influential spiritual or religious leadership can be that and the briefest of glances at history would surely suffice.

The amazing variety of religious/spiritual practices lends itself to another fascinating concept, whichever you choose to follow (or not to follow) regardless of culture, identity, gender, location or even social status according to many religious texts these factors are regarded as irrelevant. That must bring great comfort to anyone regardless of their own religious or non-religious beliefs. What could be argued (as it usually is) is that personal spiritual experiences can provide peace of mind combined with profound personal insights.

God (or at least the concept of god) is there for all to reflect upon and whether you believe, have faith or not it is always our actions and not mere words on which moral validity is based and measured. Philosophers and others have spoken and written about the idea of our higher selves, could that also be seen as an example of our true potential in all things?

4
Politics

Many in this world find it totally unbelievable that large sections of the human population can be coerced so easily. How did we as a collective of individuals allow ourselves to be controlled (or manipulated) in this way? The answer is sadly too easy to see, but not easy to acknowledge as the present human condition is one of ignorance and apathy combined with a lack of self-honesty and critical thought.

The hardest thing for any individual to do at any time is to disagree with others (in whole or in part) when so many have already convinced themselves or have been convinced by others (regarding policies) through shallow talking points, empty slogans and propaganda. Every tactic is used from intimidation, imprisonment, and even killing to suppress or deny ideas that challenge the legitimacy and integrity of leaders and/or their policies.

In the twisted arena of politics, the most deviant and selfish aspects of human behaviour have been given free reign (and rewards) to mislead humanity down a path of scarcity, conflict and curtailed potential. The dangers in this regard cannot be underestimated as the idea that a few can guide the many to a brighter future is an illusion created and perpetuated by those who wish to gain the most from that future while making the most from the present for themselves.

The fact that many have allowed this to happen and continue to occur is a huge concern for an ever-growing percentage of the populations of many nations. And it seems like during times of upheaval be it of a social, environmental, political or financial form, when an overwhelming majority have grievances with their leaders all that is usually offered is more lies, deceit or violence to maintain their cruel and unjust authority.

The instability being witnessed around our world is merely an old system being denounced by those who have suffered or felt excluded the most as a result of these systems being implemented and continued. What is now becoming more undeniable is that an ever growing cross section of people are getting involved with demonstrations or protests (and counter protests) which all too often result in violent and destructive behaviour which belittles any injustice being fought against (agent provocateurs have been blamed at times for this), an honest and open debate is becoming more critical as the level of frustration and violence continues to grow.

With the rise and growth of what have been called "hate groups" or "radical extremists religious/political groups" the chances for peace are becoming harder to find with violence used to justify more violence. When any supposed revolution uses violence isn't it reasonable to assume that violence will be used to achieve its goals, to also promote itself, to also resist against it and to also maintain control of those involved within it regardless of its moral direction (or lack of) regarding its leadership? These dangers cannot be ignored as any of us can be victims, perpetrators or witnesses of this misery. If politics has taught us anything, can it be that a promise not delivered upon is worth nothing and could even be viewed as an accurate definition of a lie?

5
Health

The balance and vitality within and between mind and body is the foundation of all human (and every other biological entity's) potential. No person, regardless of their social status, age, gender, intelligence, ethnicity or religion is immune from the debilitating effects of ill health (both mental and physical injury) one of the most revealing aspects of human society is that if you are born into the lower classes of any state, country or region, your overall mental and physical well-being is the most profoundly affected aspect of your existence.

Even in developed nations with universal (or some refer to it as socialised) heath care the lifespan and overall quality of life is significantly reduced for a considerable percentage of the population. This usually manifests itself as strained and overcrowded hospitals combined with a loss of revenue and production (both personal and national) through sickness.

When viewed globally the imbalance of available nutrition as well as a lack of clean drinking water and the shortage (or non-existence) of basic health care facilities being a concern for a considerable percentage of the worlds people the future seems needlessly bleak. With the developed world witnessing ever increasing amounts of obesity and other eating disorders leading to unnecessary and debilitating physical and psychological complaints while the developing world suffer from increasing rates of starvation, malnutrition combined with a lack of infrastructure to counteract the problems of poverty, hunger and disease, it's becoming clear that the social and medical systems of both sides of the issues need new solutions. The social and moral implications that this imbalance has for our species cannot be underestimated. As an example no one would expect a seed from a plant to reach its full potential (therefore its chance to live, grow and reproduce) without the nutritional input of soil and water combined with the energy from the sun. From this example alone is it reasonable to conclude that only the most cruel and selfish attitudes of humankind would deny that potential to any living organism?

This can all of course be considered trivial when we consider the health and vitality of our planet as a whole. With scientists and researchers expressing dire warnings regarding our actions towards the natural world (these have included such things as volcanic events, solar activity as well as human activities such as de-forestation and industrial pollutants etc) the cumulative effects that these alone pose to our farming, manufacturing, infrastructure and housing while also threatening the habitats, air quality and food sources of every other creature on our planet are not to be ignored.

It's more apparent than ever that our actions are increasingly damaging our health and well-being in ways which have the ability to alarm (but also inspire) anyone with the courage to face them and the willingness to assist in resolving them. When any individual feels positive about themselves they naturally feel the same about others and their surrounding environment. Someone who feels negatively will usually act in the opposite way by hurting themselves and others (or at best feel indifferent) and also their environment. This in itself asks the question "how do you feel?"

6
Sexuality

Love and its closely related emotional states such as lust, jealousy etc are expressed in all ways by human beings (and have also been observed in many other species) nowadays, sexuality (alongside race and religion) is used as rather a weak excuse to pass judgement on an individual or entire groups, with sexuality (and all its sins/virtues) being a common topic of discussion amongst many political, spiritual and other social groups it's quite shameful to observe that bigotry is being allowed to influence debate or any possibility of consensus being reached with these attempts being degraded into mindless name calling and presumption.

While no one could argue that laws passed to protect anyone be they man woman or child from the degrading act of sexual abuse are essential in any society, it seems a curious state of affairs that consenting adults of the same gender (who only wish to declare and celebrate their love for each other through the act of marriage) are denied that right and many others in many parts of the world for any and all reasons be they of the aforementioned religious or political reasoning.

On a more individual level many would also consider it presumptuous or just plain rude to assume another person's moral values towards any issue based on something as individualistic as sexual orientation/preference. With sexuality being used as an excuse to exclude individuals from certain professions, with the most obvious of these being the military or priesthood (though advancements towards inclusion have been achieved) the need for rational debate towards all matters regarding sexuality are being stalled by those who for whatever reason they find valid to attempt to make any discussion or progress seem irrelevant.

As gay, trans and bisexual rights have been fought for as much as any other freedom is it unreasonable to suggest that all rights/laws regarding sexual conduct be discussed in a rational and informed manner? Furthermore can all laws regarding sexual conduct be applied and enforced on a basis of equal responsibility without regard for social status, gender, gender identity, ethnicity or sexual orientation?

With the institution of marriage (as mentioned before) coming more into the spotlight in many more parts of the world with regards to same sex couples (can't love between two consenting adults be the institution?) and with other problems facing all of humanity (pollution, corruption, economic instability, poverty, war and famine etc) it's becoming ever more important that all these issues are faced with compassion and reason and not divisive protests.

On a more individual level is it not reasonable to consider that if any society, culture or country would deny even the most basic rights and dignity to one section of the community are they likely to deny or endeavour to take away any other rights from everyone or anyone else?

7
War

Out of all human behaviour, nothing at any time or anywhere has caused more depletion of natural resources and division of generations of people and cultures than the act of war. It's been said many times that "war is a hungry beast that devours everything in its path." No statement or quote has described this insanity in such a profound way, yet for so many problems in our world it's put forward by so many and so often as the only solution. If war is hell it's a hell of our own making.

No nation at any time that has increased its military capability has ever kept this additional capacity within its own borders. The only time when this capacity has remained within a nation is when it has been used to oppress that nation's own population usually manifesting as civil war, authoritarian rule and genocide. As any empire expands its armies have always grown with it, and when no more arms, troops and other resources can be sought in the empire's home state, all additional materials and troops etc. are brought in on a mercenary or by a violent conquest basis to further the selfish desires of the empire's builders. What is most revealing is that the vast percentage of the empire's home states citizens are kept passive and compliant by being told (through propaganda) that all sacrifices whether in loss or restrictions of civil liberties, family members, financial strain or property, combined with the destruction being performed in their name is done to benefit them.

The truth is that they benefit the least (while sacrificing the most) when compared to their leaders. How soul destroying and alarming it is to see that for centuries the same social structures and attitudes that have built (and in many cases destroyed) countries and empires are still with us in today's world. Is this a risk that we as human beings are willing to take?

How can it be that when groups or individuals that are (and sadly continue to be) unfairly labelled as unpatriotic, pacifistic, cowardly or even defeatist when raising doubts of the validity of violent actions (particularly regarding foreign interventions) are always treated with misplaced suspicion and yet are rarely ever debated fairly, but are usually censored or ignored entirely? How can this be when as children we are generally taught not to hurt others and to always tell the truth? Do we forget these teachings so easily or are we just denying ourselves of their moral value?

If war can be defined as "the absence of peace" then surely peace can be defined as "the absence of war"? Through all the destruction and misery that our past and present continue to show us, it must also contain the capacity to express our most serious of choices, whether or not to continue this path or to choose a new one. This choice is not the sole domain of leaders, it's a moral choice for everyone to make. Many people are hoping (and striving) for a positive change and new direction for the future, for if the future is a product of these choices then the only advice or guidance anyone can give to another is to choose wisely, as a past and present based on conflict will surely guarantee a future of further violence.

Where do we go from here?
WAR
PEACE
DISEASE
CURE
POVERTY
WEALTH
SCARCITY
ABUNDANCE
MISERY
HAPPINESS
LIES
TRUTH

8
Four Examples of Truth and Hope

Dr Martin Luther King: Anti-Vietnam war speech, Riverside church, New York April 4th, 1967

A true revolution of values will lay hand on the world order and say of war "This way of settling differences is not just." This business of burning human beings with napalm, of filling our nations homes with orphans and widows, of injecting poisonous drugs of hate into the veins of people normally humane, or sending men home from dark and bloody battlefields physically handicapped and psychologically deranged, cannot be reconciled with wisdom, justice and love. A nation that continues year after year to spend more money on military defense than it does on programs of social uplift is approaching spiritual death.

Beyond Vietnam: A time to break silence.
https://kingandbreakingsilence.org/dr-king-speech/

John Fitzgerald Kennedy: Speech before the American Newspaper Publishers Association April 27th, 1961

The very word "secrecy" is repugnant in a free and open society, and we are as people inherently and historically opposed to secret societies, to secret oaths and to secret proceedings. We decided long ago that the dangers of excessive and unwarranted concealment of pertinent facts far outweigh the dangers which are cited to justify it. Even today, there is little value in opposing the threat of a closed society by imitating its arbitrary restrictions. Even today there is little value in ensuring the survival of our nation if our traditions do not survive with it.

And there is very grave danger that an announced need for increased security will be seized upon by those anxious to expand its meaning to the very limits of official censorship and concealment. That I do not intend to permit to the extent that is in my control. And no official of my Administration, whether his rank is high or low, civilian or military should interpret my words tonight as an excuse to censor the news, to stifle dissent, to cover up our mistakes or to withhold from the press and the public the facts they deserve to know.

The President and the Press found at:
https://www.jfklibrary.org/archives/other-resources/john-f-kennedy-speeches/american-newspaper-publishers-association-19610427

Malcolm X: Oxford Union Debate December 3rd, 1964

I read once passingly about a man named Shakespeare, I only read about him passingly, but I remember one thing he wrote that kind of moved me. He put it in the mouth of Hamlet I think it was who said "To be or not to be." He was in doubt about something - whether it was nobler in the minds of man to suffer the slings and arrows of outrageous fortune - moderation - or to take up arms against a sea of troubles and by opposing end them. And I go for that, if you take up arms you'll end it, but if you sit around and wait for the one who's in power to make up his mind that he should end it, you'll be waiting a long time. And in my opinion, the young generation of whites, blacks, browns, whatever else there is, you're living at a time of extremism, a time of revolution, a time when there's got to be a change. People in power have misused it, and now there has to be a change and a better world has to be built, and the only way it's going to be built is with extreme methods. And I for one will join in with anyone I don't care what colour you are as long as you want to change this miserable condition that exists on this earth. Thank you.

1964: Malcolm X Evokes Shakespeare at The Oxford Union
https://flashbak.com/1964-malcolm-x-evokes-shakespeare-as-he-thrills-the-oxford-union-with-talk-of-armed-rebellion-10810/

Jacque Fresco: (Co-founder of The Venus Project)
From the documentary: Zeitgeist Moving Forward

When I was a young man growing up in New York City, I refused to pledge allegiance to the flag. Of course, I was sent to the principal's office and he asked me "why don't you want to pledge allegiance? Everybody does" I said, "everybody once believed the Earth was flat, but that doesn't make it so." I explained that America owed everything it has to other cultures and other nations, and that I would rather pledge allegiance to the Earth and everyone on it. Needless to say it wasn't long before I left school entirely and I set up a lab in my bedroom. There I began to learn about science and nature. I realised then that the universe was governed by laws, and that the human being along with society itself was not exempt from these laws.

Then came the crash of 1929 which began what we now call 'The Great Depression.' I found it difficult to understand why millions were out of work, homeless, starving while all the factories were sitting there the resources were unchanged. It was then that I realised that the rules of the economic game were inherently invalid.

Shortly after came World War 2, where various nations took turns systematically destroying each other. I later calculated that all the destruction and wasted resources spent on that war could have easily provided for every human need on the planet. Since that time I have watched humanity set the stage for its own extinction. I have watched as the precious finite resources are perpetually wasted and destroyed in the name of profit and free markets. I have watched the social values of society be reduced into a base artificiality of materialism and mindless consumption. And I have watched as the monetary powers control the political structure of supposedly free societies. I'm 94 years old now and I'm afraid my disposition is the same as it was 75 years ago.

"This shit's got to go."

Zeitgeist: Moving Forward (Transcript)
https://scrapsfromtheloft.com/movies/zeitgeist-moving-forward-transcript/

9
A Most Unlikely/Unusual Manifesto

Foreign Policy and Defence

All military personnel, equipment, supplies, vehicles, munitions and weapons returned to country of origin.
All foreign military bases closed.
All use of drones banned.
All foreign arms sales banned.
All manufacturing of landmines, biological, chemical and nuclear weapons (included depleted uranium munitions) banned.
All nuclear weapons and delivery systems dismantled.
Armed forces used only for common defence.

New peace and trade agreements to be made with all countries willing to promote peace and trade in peacetime goods only.
Creation of new open-source intelligence agency/department to reduce and eventually end the need for covert operations.
Creation of new open-source engineering agency/department to design and implement patent free technologies domestically and worldwide. These will take the form of projects to include permaculture/farming, energy generation, habitat restoration, housing, health care, education, water and sewerage treatment and desalination etc.

Creation of new international volunteer service to assist with open-source engineering projects domestically and worldwide.

Energy and Environment

All nuclear power plants de-commissioned.

No permits for future nuclear plants to be issued.

Full countrywide implementation of localised renewable energy sources including geothermal, wind solar, wave, tidal, hydroelectric and household waste and sewage incineration utilising particulate filtration and gas separation with priority given to remove the most prevalent and potent greenhouse gases (carbon dioxide, methane, nitrous oxide etc) to improve overall air quality.

Creation of new scientific/engineering department for the study of long-term nuclear waste treatment and storage.

Countrywide re-planting/preservation of all forest/woodlands, meadows, hedgerows etc. to enhance habitat for wildlife.

Countrywide waterway restoration (streams, lakes, ponds, rivers and canals) to improve soil/water quality and wildlife habitats while also reducing flooding risks.

Coastline preservation wherever possible with fishing permits/licences granted for local, seasonal traditional sustainable fishing methods.

Hydraulic fracturing (Fracking) banned.

All new construction projects to include rainwater capture and storage for additional flood protection and collection during times of drought.

Complete ban on the use of landfill with future plans to mine past and present sites for incineration (energy capture) and recyclable materials for domestic manufacture or export while bringing further improvements to soil and ground water quality.

Full use and incentives to utilise all industrial hemp products including fuel, lubricants, clothing, construction materials, plastics, health products etc.

All publicly owned (taxpayer funded) renewable energy to be priced to cover initial installation, wages and maintenance costs only.

Health

Universal health care for all citizens covering all aspects of human health focusing primarily on prevention and early as possible diagnosis of health problems.
Optional yearly health checks for all citizens.
Nutrition studies included in all physical education school programmes with a minimum of 3 hours physical activity and 1-hour minimum nutritional study per week.
All GMO's (products, crops, additives, seeds etc) banned.
Full review and independent study and testing of all natural and artificial colours, flavourings, sweeteners, preservatives etc. with immediate bans or significant reductions of use of any with a reasonable potential to harm human health.
Fluoridation of all water supplies banned.
Independent testing of all vaccines to protect public health.
All ingredients without exception listed on all vaccines packaging.
Nutrition information made available across all health services to help prevent the onset of chronic illness (arthritis, heart disease, high/low blood pressure etc) this can help reduce dependency on prescription drugs wherever possible.

Drugs Policy

Full legislation of all cannabis/marijuana products.
Registration of all retailers and producers.
Strict enforced minimum age of 18 years for alcohol, tobacco and cannabis/marijuana purchases and consumption.

Fines, imprisonment and property confiscation for the sale of any intoxicants to anyone under 18 years of age.

Flat rate fines (and optional treatment in extreme cases of addiction) for all illegal drug possession cases.

Normal arrest and court procedures for illegal substance possession, sale, production, trafficking.

All revenues from fines from illegal drug sales/importation and possession as well as property confiscations and the revenues from legal sales of alcohol, tobacco and cannabis used to fund a comprehensive drugs/alcohol treatment programme.

Programme to Include:

Relevant information regarding risks to mental and physical health made available to school children aged 14 years old and over.

Free assistance for any citizen suffering from addiction to any substance including:

> Residential treatment (this will take the strain off other health services and help reduce homelessness).
>
> Medications (nicotine patches etc).
>
> Mental health care.
>
> Additional assistance regarding long term sobriety (counselling, treatment advice).
>
> Further assistance in case of future relapse.

10
So Where Do We Go From Here?

> It is easier to fool people
> than to convince them that
> they have been fooled.
>
> Attributed to Mark Twain
> 1835-1910

It's more than understandable to feel that change for the better is somehow wishful thinking when all we seem to be shown or exposed to is either disturbing, divisive, shallow, vain or trivial, especially when they are used as mere distractions to take our collective attention away from issues that endanger all of us (social inequality, instability, political and financial corruption, warfare, environmental destruction etc).

With just these issues in mind many would consider it to be highly unwise to fault anyone for having legitimate concerns for the future.

But this situation is merely an illusion (albeit a very powerful one) fed to us by a system we ourselves perpetuate with our compliance and apathy. With our world being pushed to the brink of social, environmental collapse and seemingly never-ending wars which benefit the few while all others suffer is it no surprise that an undercurrent of anger and resentment is growing?

But it doesn't have to be this way as our history shows us many times. Philosophers of the ancient world up to modern day researchers have given, and continue to give dire warnings about being unaware, apathetic or uninformed about choices being made that govern your life. At the same time, those in so called authority through all forms of media convince you and others that you are somehow not worthy or qualified to make, or participate in the making of such choices for yourself, or to even understand the information to do so. Many would consider this to be the greatest insult to our individual intelligence and dignity.

The problems we face are only as complex as we perceive or allow them to be, and this can also be said for the solutions to them. As we live in a world in which near unimaginable sums of money are spent (or wasted) on conflicts worldwide while infrastructure falls into disrepair and services (health, education etc) suffer from cuts in funding something somewhere is clearly wrong. Is it too much to consider that our present course not only endangers all of us, but it is also unsustainable, unjust and immoral?

It is the duty and the right of any human being to stand against these injustices while also to strive to see that those who profit from the misery, enslavement or exploitation of others are given the righteous punishment they deserve. But as our collective situation worsens and becomes more dire the solutions to them will themselves become more drastic which in many could breed yet more fear and apathy and will therefore delay our collective progress.

But as our fears and problems are confronted our will and courage will grow and a new era can begin in which our environment is protected, human dignity and potential are nurtured while the mistakes of the past are diligently studied so as not to repeat them. Who could possibly wish to delay such a transformation?

In Closing

The subjects that have been analysed in the previous chapters (and any others that have not) are like the systems that give us life in our world, interwoven and connected. With issues such as pollution, quality of nutrition, additives in food, genetic modification of crops and mistreatment of farm animals in general and the never-ending conflicts of both individual countries and international affairs, can any individual be blamed for having concerns for the future?

Our choices, actions and inactions have guided the world to its present-day conditions and therefore our choices and actions can also change it for the benefit of not just the human condition, but also for that of all other creatures and the planet itself. No one person has all the answers, but cooperation between the many will greatly improve the chances of finding solutions. Human suffering can never be removed from the world, but our collective understanding of its causes and the compassion to give care and support to those that are victims of its results are limitless.

A future in which poverty, war, slavery and cruelty no longer exist is possible, it is only a matter of choice and action to bring it to fruition. With our modern world drowning us in triviality and inane controversy while our world is increasingly poisoned and destroyed, a new direction is needed more than ever. As for this brighter future, our human dignity demands it, our imaginations can foresee it and our aforementioned choices and actions can produce it. What a joyful journey that could be.